DESIGN

bedrooms • dormitorios • chambres • schlafzimmer

authors
fernando de haro & omar fuentes

editorial design & production

EDITORES   PUBLISHERS

project managers
edali nuñez daniel
laura mijares castellá

coordination
ana teresa vázquez de la mora

copywriter
roxana villalobos waisbord

english translation
babel international translators sc

french translation
julia sánchez rojo

german translation
angloamericano de cuernavaca
sabine klein

prepress coordination
carolina medina granados

design • inside
bedrooms • dormitorios • chambres • schlafzimmer

printed in thailand.

index
índice

introduction

introducción • introduction • einleitung

ntroduction

Of all the different spaces in a house, the bedroom is the stronghold of intimacy pc xcellence. This book explores three basic aspects to be taken into account in interior desig and bedrooms: texture, style and peacefulness .

Texture is defined by the outer surfaces of objects and their finishes; it's the first thing the reveal to us, be it through sight or tact. The human perceptive memory possesses a serie of properties associated with texture. Silk and velvet, for instance, are associated wit softness, wool with warmth, metals with coldness, and the list goes on. These perception are projected as part of the setting depending on one's decision regarding bedroom déco Style is not just a mere reflection of a particular decorative trend. In the case of a bedroom space is expressed through the personal touch of its occupant. This is where his or he preferences, tastes, personality, perceptions and habits are manifested.

For example, the headrest of a bed with integrated cushioning is usually a good option fc people who like to read in bed, while headrests made of wood or other materials tend perform a more decorative role.

Then there is the topic of peacefulness. Good performance in life requires restful sleep a settings that evoke tranquility, make for nourishing sleep and allow relaxation. A fe simple and practical tips will help achieve this. The important thing is to be aware of th behavior of the combination of textures, style, the use of color, light and the practicality c the furniture. All of these components are crucial when it comes to setting the bedroom ambience, while its balance is essential for creating spatial harmony

introducción

De los espacios de una casa, la recámara es por excelencia el albergue de la intimidad. Este libro relata tres aspectos esenciales a considerar en el interiorismo y de un dormitorio: textura, estilo y tranquilidad.

La textura es la propiedad que poseen las superficies externas de los objetos, su acabado; es lo primero que percibimos de éstos, ya sea a través de la vista o del tacto. Hay en la memoria perceptiva del ser humano una serie de propiedades asociadas con las texturas. Por ejemplo, a la seda y al terciopelo se les relaciona con la suavidad, a la lana con la calidez, a los metales con el frío, entre un largo etcétera. Estas percepciones conforman parte del ambiente que se transmite al decidir decorar una habitación de una u otra manera.

Por su cuenta, el estilo no se refiere meramente a alguna corriente decorativa, en el caso de un dormitorio, en la expresión del espacio está contenido el toque personal de quien lo habita; allí se alojan sus preferencias, gustos, forma de ser y de sentir, y se evidencian sus hábitos.

Por ejemplo, los respaldos de una cama con almohadones incorporados, generalmente representan una opción para quienes aprovechan la cama como lugar de lectura, en tanto que aquellos hechos de madera y otros materiales tienen generalmente fines propiamente decorativos.

Por último, el tema de la tranquilidad. Para tener un buen desempeño es necesario dormir tranquilos en atmósferas que evoquen paz, permitan sueños regeneradores y ayuden a la relajación. Para conseguirlo existen algunos consejos prácticos y sencillos que es necesario implementar. Lo más importante es sentir el comportamiento que tienen la combinación de texturas, el estilo, el uso del color, la luz y la funcionalidad del mobiliario. Todos éstos se convierten en elementos medulares del efecto anímico que desprenda el dormitorio y su balance y equilibrio son fundamentales para la armonía espacial.

Parmi les pièces de la maison, la chambre à coucher est celle de l'intime par excellence. Cet ouvrage aborde trois aspects qu'il est essentiel de prendre en compte si l'on souhaite décorer une chambre : la texture, le style et la sensation de tranquillité.

La texture désigne les propriétés que possèdent les surfaces externes d'un objet, sa finition: c'est la première chose que nous percevons, par la vue ou le toucher. Et la mémoire perceptive de l'être humain associe un certain nombre de propriétés à ces textures. Par exemple, la soie et le velours nous font penser à la douceur, la laine à la chaleur, les métaux au froid, etc. Ces perceptions jouent un rôle dans l'atmosphère dégagée par la chambre et il est important d'y réfléchir lorsque l'on opte pour telle ou telle décoration.

Le style, quant à lui, n'est pas simplement l'expression d'une tendance décorative précise. Dans une chambre à coucher, la touche personnelle des personnes qui l'utilisent modifie également l'atmosphère de la pièce. Cet espace exprime alors leurs préférences, leurs goûts, reflète leur façon d'être, de ressentir les choses et leurs habitudes.

Une tête de lit, par exemple, avec de gros oreillers, est en général un bon choix pour tous ceux qui aiment lire au lit. Et une tête de lit fabriquée en bois et avec d'autres matériaux est souvent très riche en tant qu'élément décoratif.

Pour finir, parlons de la tranquillité. Pour mener une existence satisfaisante, il est important de bien dormir, dans une pièce qui respire le calme, afin de profiter d'un sommeil réparateur et de bien se relaxer. Il est essentiel de suivre quelques conseils simples et pratiques pour bénéficier d'une telle chambre. Le plus important consiste à bien évaluer l'association entre les textures, le style, l'utilisation des couleurs, la lumière et les fonctions du mobilier. Tous ces éléments jouent un rôle primordial sur le moral des personnes qui utilisent la chambre et il est nécessaire d'atteindre un certain

Von allen Räumen des Hauses ist das Schlafzimmer der Ort der Intimität schlechthin. Dieses Buch behandelt drei wesentliche Aspekte, die bei der Innendekoration und einem Schlafzimmers zu beachten sind: Textur, Stil und Klarheit.

Textur ist die Eigenschaft der Oberflächen der Objekte, seine Verarbeitung; sie ist das erste, was wir von ihnen wahrnehmen, sei es mit den Augen oder durch Berührung. Im Gedächtnis des Menschen sind eine Reihe mit Texturen verknüpfte Assoziationen gespeichert. Zum Beispiel verbindet man Samt und Seide mit Sanftheit, Wolle mit Wärme, Metalle mit Kälte und vieles vieles mehr. Diese Wahrnehmungen bilden Teil des Ambientes, dass man mit der Entscheidung einen Raum in der einen oder anderen Weise zu dekorieren, vermittelt.

Was den Stil betrifft, geht es nicht ausschliesslich um irgendeine Tendenz in der Dekoration, im Fall eines Schlafzimmers, im Eindruck des Raumes, ist der persönliche Anstrich der Bewohner mit inbegriffen; dort finden sich seine Vorzüge, sein Geschmack, seine Art zu sein und zu fühlen und es zeigen sich seine Gewohnheiten.

Zum Beispiel repräsentieren die Rückenlehnen eines Bettes mit integrierten Kissen normalerweise eine Option für diejenigen, die das Bett als Ort zum Lesen nutzen, während jene, die aus Holz und anderen Materialien gefertigt sind, normalerweise rein dekorativ sind. Als letztes das Thema Klarheit. Für gute Leistung ist es notwendig ruhig zu schlafen, in einer Atmosphäre die Frieden ausstrahlt, erholsamen Schlaf ermöglicht und bei der Entspannung hilft. Um das zu erreichen gibt es einige praktische und einfache Ratschläge, die umgesetzt werden sollten. Am wichtigsten ist es, den Effekt der Kombination von Textur, Stil, Farbe, Licht und Möbel, zu spüren. All dies wird zu einem entscheidenden Faktor für die Auswirkung auf die Stimmung, die ein Schlafzimmer ausstrahlt und ihre Ausgewogenheit und ihr Gleichgewicht sind grundlegend für eine räumliche Harmonie.

texture

textura • texture • textur

IN ORDER FOR A SPACE TO LOOK IN HARMONY, THE TEXTURES OF
CURTAINS, CARPETS, UPHOLSTERY, BED LINEN, WALL SURFACES
AND FURNITURE NEED TO BE BALANCED.

PARA QUE UN ESPACIO LUZCA ARMÓNICO
LAS TEXTURAS DE CORTINAS, ALFOMBRAS,
TAPICES, ROPA DE CAMA, ACABADOS DE
PAREDES Y MUEBLES TIENEN QUE ESTAR
EQUILIBRADAS.

POUR QUE LA CHAMBRE SOIT
HARMONIEUSE, LES TEXTURES DE
RIDEAUX, DE LA MOQUETTE, DES TAPIS,
DE LA LITERIE AINSI QUE LA SURFACE DES
MURS ET DES MEUBLES DOIVENT ÊTRE
ÉQUILIBRÉES.

DAMIT EIN RAUM HARMONISCH WIRKT,
MUSS DIE TEXTUR DER VORHÄNGE,
TEPPICHE, TAPETEN, BETTWÄSCHE,
WANDOBERFLÄCHEN UND MÖBEL IM
GLEICHGEWICHT STEHEN.

THE BED IS THE BEDROOM'S PROTAGONIST, WHICH MEANS THE EIDERDOWN, PILLOWS AND HEADREST WILL PERFORM A MAJOR ROLE IN SETTING THE OVERALL TONE.

LA CAMA ES LA PROTAGONISTA DEL DORMITORIO, POR LO QUE LAS TRAMAS DE SUS EDREDONES, ALMOHADONES, Y CABECERA INCIDEN EN LA IMPRESIÓN DE LA ATMÓSFERA GENERAL.

LE LIT A LE RÔLE LE PLUS IMPORTANT DANS UNE CHAMBRE. LES TISSUS UTILISÉS POUR LA COUETTE, LES OREILLERS ET LE CHEVET CONTRIBUENT DONC GRANDEMENT À L'ATMOSPHÈRE GÉNÉRALE DE LA PIÈCE.

DAS BETT SPIELT DIE HAUPTROLLE IM SCHLAFZIMMER, WESWEGEN DAS ZUSAMMENSPIEL SEINER DECKEN, KISSEN UND DES KOPFTEILES EINE ENTSCHEIDENDE ROLLE FÜR DIE ALLGEMEINE ATMOSPHÄRE SPIELEN.

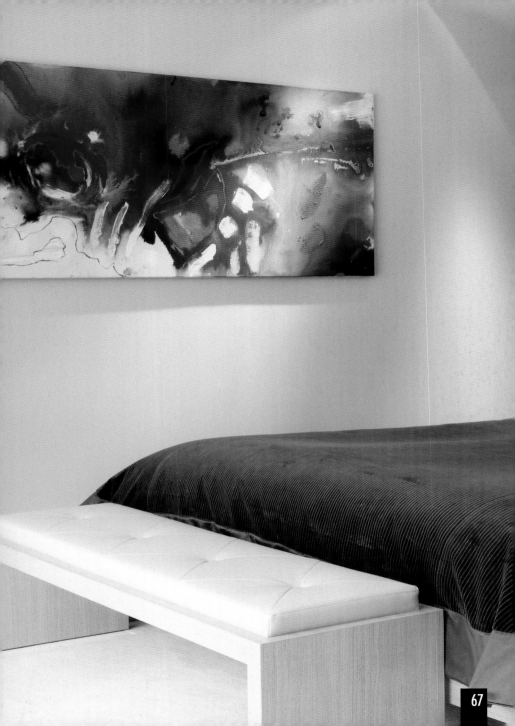

HIGHLY TEXTURED CLOTH DOMINATED BY RELIEVES AND PATTERNS INFUSE THE BEDROOM WITH PERSONALITY AND HELP PROVIDE IT WITH A TOUCH OF ORIGINALITY.

LAS TELAS MUY TEXTURIZADAS, EN LAS QUE PREDOMINAN LOS RELIEVES Y DIBUJOS, DOTAN DE PERSONALIDAD Y AYUDAN A DARLE UN TOQUE ORIGINAL A LA HABITACIÓN.

LES TISSUS TRÈS TRAVAILLÉS, AVEC DES MOTIFS ET EN RELIEF, PERSONNALISENT LA CHAMBRE À COUCHER ET APPORTENT UN PEU D'ORIGINALITÉ DANS LA PIÈCE.

STOFFE MIT STARKER TEXTUR, IN DENEN RELIEFS UND ZEICHNUNGEN VORHERRSCHEN, GEBEN PERSÖNLICHKEIT UND HELFEN DEM ZIMMER EINEN ORIGINELLEN ANSTRICH ZU GEBEN.

SOFT TEXTURES ARE IDEAL FOR DEFINING A BEDROOM'S AMBIENCE. THEY ARE SOFT TO THE TOUCH AND AFFORD A FEELING OF FIRMNESS.

FAVORECE A LA ATMÓSFERA DE UNA RECÁMARA EL DOMINIO DE LAS TEXTURAS SUAVES, ADEMÁS DE SER SENSUALES AL TACTO, VISUALMENTE DAN LA SENSACIÓN DE TERSURA.

LES TEXTURES DOUCES ET SENSUELLES AU TOUCHER, TRANSFORMENT UNE CHAMBRE EN LIEU DOUILLET ET SONT TOUT INDIQUÉES POUR L'ATMOSPHÈRE DE CETTE PIÈCE.

DIE ATMOSPHÄRE WIRD DURCH DIE VORHERRSCHAFT VON SANFTEN TEXTUREN BEGÜNSTIGT, DAVON ABGESEHEN, DASS SIE SICH SINNLICH ANFÜHLEN, VERMITTELN SIE OPTISCH DEN EINDRUCK VON GLÄTTE.

style

estilo • style • stil

THE BEDROOM IS THE MOST INTIMATE PART OF THE HOUSE. IT IS WHERE TASTES AND PREFERENCES ARE EXPRESSED, WHICH MAKES IT THE IDEAL SETTING FOR WORKS OF ART, RELIGIOUS IMAGES, PHOTOS AND MEMOIRS.

LA HABITACIÓN ES EL LUGAR MÁS ÍNTIMO, ALBERGA LAS AFICIONES Y PREFERENCIAS, POR LO QUE ES IDÓNEO PARA PIEZAS DE ARTE, IMÁGENES RELIGIOSAS, FOTOGRAFÍAS Y RECUERDOS.

LA CHAMBRE EST LA PIÈCE LA PLUS INTIME DE LA MAISON. C'EST L'ENDROIT PARFAIT POUR Y EXPRIMER SES GOÛTS ET SES PRÉFÉRENCES AVEC DES OBJETS D'ART, DES MOTIFS RELIGIEUX, DES PHOTOS, DES SOUVENIRS.

DAS SCHLAFZIMMER IST DER INTIMSTE RAUM, ER BEHERBERGT DIE NEIGUNGEN UND VORLIEBEN, WODURCH ER IDEAL FÜR KUNSTWERKE, RELIGIÖSE ABBILDUNGEN, FOTOS UND ANDENKEN IST.

A GOOD WAY TO CREATE A PEACEFUL ATMOSPHERE IS BY USING A SIMPLE DESIGN BASED ON STRAIGHT-LINED SHAPES AND A LIMITED RANGE OF MATERIALS.

PARA PROVOCAR UNA ATMÓSFERA APACIBLE HAY QUE LIMITARSE A UN DISEÑO SIMPLE, BASADO EN FORMAS RECTAS Y UNA SELECCIÓN DE MATERIALES REDUCIDA.

POUR DONNER À LA CHAMBRE UNE ATMOSPHÈRE CALME, IL FAUT SE LIMITER À UN DESIGN SIMPLE À BASE DE FORMES DROITES ET DE MATÉRIAUX EN NOMBRE RESTREINT.

UM EINE BESCHAULICHE ATMOSPHÄRE ZU SCHAFFEN SOLLTE MAN SICH AUF EIN SCHLICHTES DESIGN BESCHRÄNKEN, DAS AUF GERADE FORMEN UND EINE BESCHRÄNKE AUSWAHL AN MATERIALIEN BERUHT.

COMPLEMENTARY FURNITURE SUCH AS, LOVE SEATS, CHAISE LONGS AND BENCHES IS USEFUL WHEN IT COMES TO READING, WATCHING TV OR HAVING A CHAT.

EL MOBILIARIO COMPLEMENTARIO COMO SILLONES, LOVE SEATS, CHAISE LONGS Y BANCAS ES MUY ÚTIL PARA LEER, VER TELE O TENER UNA CONVERSACIÓN.

LE MOBILIER D'APPOINT COMME LES FAUTEUILS, LOVESEATS, CHAISES LONGUES ET AUTRES TABOURETS EST TRÈS UTILE POUR LIRE, REGARDER LA TÉLÉ OU BAVARDER.

ZUSÄTZLICHE MÖBEL, WIE SESSEL, ZWEISITZER, CHAISE LONGS UND BÄNKE SIND NÜTZLICH ZUM LESEN, ZUM FERNSEHEN ODER UM GESPRÄCHE ZU FÜHREN.

THE BEDROOM'S FOCAL POINTS CAN BE DEFINED BE USING LARGE, ATTENTION-GRABBING OBJECTS, SUCH AS PAINTINGS, RUGS OR THE SURROUNDING NATURE.

LOS PUNTOS FOCALES DE UNA RECÁMARA SE CONSIGUEN INCLUYENDO PIEZAS LLAMATIVAS DE GRAN FORMATO, PUEDE SER UN CUADRO, UN TAPETE, O LA PROPIA NATURALEZA CIRCUNDANTE.

POUR QU'UNE CHAMBRE COMPRENNE DES POINTS DE MIRE, IL FAUT FAIRE RESSORTIR DES OBJETS DE GRAND FORMAT QUI ATTIRENT L'ŒIL COMME UN TABLEAU, UN TAPIS OU, POURQUOI PAS, LA VUE SUR LA VÉGÉTATION EXTÉRIEURE.

BLICKFÄNGE IN EINEM SCHLAFZIMMER SCHAFFT MAN, IN DEM MAN AUFFÄLLIGE STÜCKE IN GROSSEM FORMAT MIT EINBEZIEHT, DAS KANN EIN GEMÄLDE SEIN, EIN TEPPICH ODER DIE UMGEBENDE NATUR SELBST.

peaceful

tranquilidad • tranquillité • gelassenheit

WINDOWS, MIRRORS, TRANSPARENCIES AND LIGHTS ARE THINGS
THAT MODEL SPACE AND REGULATE LIGHT. THEY CAN ALSO PROVIDE
A RELAXED SETTING ANY TIME OF THE DAY.

VENTANAS, ESPEJOS, TRANSPARENCIAS
Y LUMINARIAS SON ELEMENTOS
MODELADORES DEL ESPACIO Y
REGULADORES DE LA LUZ, CON LOS QUE
SE PUEDE LOGRAR UN CLIMA RELAJADO
A CADA HORA DEL DÍA.

LES FENÊTRES, LES MIROIRS, LES OBJETS
TRANSPARENTS ET LES LUMINAIRES, QUI
MODÈLENT L'ESPACE ET MODIFIENT LA
LUMIÈRE, FONT DE LA CHAMBRE UN LIEU
DE DÉTENTE À TOUS MOMENTS DE LA
JOURNÉE.

FENSTER, SPIEGEL, DURCHSICHTIGES
UND LEUCHTEN SIND ELEMENTE, DIE
DEN RAUM FORMEN UND DAS LICHT
REGULIEREN, MIT DENEN MAN ZU JEDER
TAGESZEIT EIN ENTSPANNTES KLIMA
HERSTELLEN KANN.

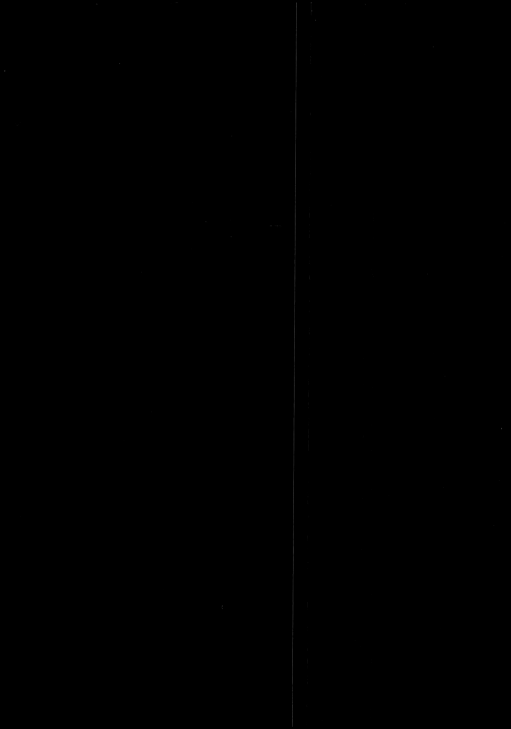

WHITE EXUDES PEACEFULNESS AND ORDER. WHEN COMBINED WITH OTHER NEUTRAL TONES, IT MODIFIES THEIR BRILLIANCE BUT WITHOUT UNDERMINING THESE QUALITIES.

EL BLANCO TRANSMITE EL EFECTO DE ORDEN Y PAZ; SU MEZCLA CON OTROS TONOS NEUTROS MODIFICA SU LUMINOSIDAD, SIN QUE PIERDA ESTOS ATRIBUTOS.

LE BLANC DONNE UNE IMPRESSION D'ORDRE ET DE CALME. SI ON LE MÉLANGE AVEC D'AUTRES TEINTES NEUTRES, LA LUMINOSITÉ EN EST MODIFIÉE SANS QUE L'AMBIANCE CHANGE.

WEISS VERMITTELT DEN EINDRUCK VON ORDNUNG UND FRIEDEN; DIE MISCHUNG MIT ANDEREN NEUTRALEN FARBTÖNEN VERÄNDERT SEINE HELLIGKEIT OHNE DIESE EIGENSCHAFTEN ZU VERLIEREN.

MINIMALISM IS CHARACTERIZED BY SIMPLE FORMS, THE ABSENCE OF DECORATIONS AND A MINIMAL PRESENCE OF OBJECTS. THE FEWER OBJECTS THERE ARE, THE MORE SERENE THE SETTING WILL BE.

EL MINIMALISMO SE CARACTERIZA POR LAS FORMAS SIMPLES, AUSENCIA DE ADORNOS Y MÍNIMA PRESENCIA DE OBJETOS. CUANTO MENOS HAYA, MÁS SERENO SE PERCIBE EL AMBIENTE.

LE MINIMALISME EST CARACTÉRISÉ PAR DES FORMES SIMPLES, PAR UNE ABSENCE DE DÉTAILS DÉCORATIFS ET PAR UN NOMBRE RÉDUIT D'OBJETS. MOINS IL Y EN A ET PLUS LA CHAMBRE AURA L'AIR CALME.

DER MINIMALISMUS ZEICHNET SICH DURCH SCHLICHTE FORMEN AUS, DIE ABWESENHEIT VON VERZIERUNGEN UND DIE MINIMALE PRÄSENZ VON OBJEKTEN. JE WENIGER ES GIBT, UMSO RUHIGER WIRD DAS AMBIENTE EMPFUNDEN.

GRAY IS A TONE THAT CAN BE USED ON EXTENSIVE SURFACES
TO CREATE A RELAXED AMBIENCE.

EL GRIS ES UNO DE LOS TONOS QUE
SE PUEDE APLICAR EN GRANDES
SUPERFICIES PARA OBTENER UN
AMBIENTE RELAJADO.

LE GRIS EST UNE DES COULEURS QUE
L'ON PEUT UTILISER POUR DE GRANDES
SURFACES AFIN DE TRANSFORMER LA
CHAMBRE EN ESPACE DE DÉTENTE.

GRAU IST EINER DER FARBTÖNE, DER AUF
GROSSEN FLÄCHEN VERWENDET WERDEN
KANN, UM EIN ENTSPANNTES AMBIENTE
ZU ERZIELEN.

credits

créditos • crédit • kredit

2 BCO Arquitectos, David González Blanco **8** Hasbani Arquitectos, Mayer Hasbani **14-15** KA Internacional, Margarita Solórzano **26-27** JSª, Javier Sánchez **28-29** GA Grupo Arquitectura, Daniel Álvarez F. **34-35** D+S Arquitectos, Allan Dayan A. • Sonny Sutton A. **36-37** Martínez&Sordo, Juan Salvador Martínez • Luis Martín Sordo **58-59** C-Chic, Olga Mussali H. • Sara Mizrahi E. **62-63** C-Chic, Olga Mussali H. • Sara Mizrahi E. **74-75** C Cúbica, Emilio Cabrero • Andrea Cesarman • Marco A. Coello B. **76-77** Abax, Fernando de Haro L. • Jesús Fernández S. • Omar Fuentes E. • Bertha Figueroa P. **78-79** Grupo Diarq, Gina Diez Barroso de Franklin **80-81** GA Grupo Arquitectura, Daniel Álvarez F. **82-83** MarqCó, Mariangel Álvarez • Covadonga Hernández **84-85** Elías Rizo Arquitectos, Elías Rizo **86-87** Ezequiel Farca **92-93** Concepto Residencial, José Manuel Ruíz F. **95** Grupo Der, Moisés Ramos Z. • Eugenio Eraña G. • José Julio Díaz G. **96-97** Grupo Diarq, Gina Diez Barroso de Franklin **98-99** R+G Arquitectos, Felipe C. Rodríguez R. • Ángeles Guerra de la Garza E. **100-101** Inter-Arq, David Penjos Smeke **102-103** Arco Arquitectura Contemporanea, Bernardo Lew • José Lew **104-105** Covilha, Maribel González • Mely González • Blanca González **106-107** Elías Rizo Arquitectos, Elías Rizo **108-109** Félix Blanco Arquitectura y Diseño, Félix Blanco M. **112-113** C-Chic, Olga Mussali H. • Sara Mizrahi E. **114-115** Decoré / Torbeli, María Patricia Díaz de León / Elena Talavera **116-177** Decoré Interiorismo, María Patricia Díaz de León **118-119** Ezequiel Farca **120-121** Decoré Interiorismo, Mario Hallatt Díaz de León • Mauricio Hallatt Díaz de León **122-123** Abax / Patricia de Haro, Fernando de Haro L. • Jesús Fernández S. • Omar Fuentes E. • Bertha Figueroa P. **124-125** C-Chic, Olga Mussali H. • Sara Mizrahi E. **130-131** CHK Arquitectos / Grupo LBC, Eduardo Hernández / Alfonso López Baz • Javier Calleja **134-135** GGAD, Gerardo García L. **136-137** Grupo LBC, Alfonso López Baz • Javier Calleja **142-143** Cortina y Clavé, Ana Cortina • Ignacio Clavé **150-151** Terrés, Fernando Valenzuela G. • Guillermo Valenzuela G. • Javier Valenzuela G. **154-155** Vela Ruíz Estudio, Ernesto Vela Ruíz **156** Abax, Fernando de Haro L. • Jesús Fernández S. • Omar Fuentes E. • Bertha Figueroa P. **157** GLR Arquitectos, Gilberto L. Rodríguez **160-161** Martínez&Sordo, Juan Salvador Martínez • Luis Martín Sordo **162-163** Terrés, Fernando Valenzuela G. • Guillermo Valenzuela G. • Javier Valenzuela G. **164** Ecléctica Diseño, Mónica Hernández S. **165(top)** Dupuis, Alejandra Prieto • Cecilia Prieto **(bottom)** Ecléctica Diseño, Mónica Hernández S. **166-167** Abax, Fernando de Haro L. • Jesús Fernández S. • Omar Fuentes E. • Bertha Figueroa P.

174-175 JSª, Javier Sánchez 176-177 GLR Arquitectos, Gilberto L. Rodríguez 178-179 Abax, Fernando de Haro L.

• Jesús Fernández S. • Omar Fuentes E. • Bertha Figueroa P. 184-185 Gutiérrez-Alonso Arquitectos, Ángel Alonso

Chein • Eduardo Gutiérrez Guzmán 202-203 Pascal Arquitectos, Carlos Pascal • Gerard Pascal 204-205 Extracto,

Vanessa Patiño • Robert Duarte 206-207 Grupo Diarq, Gina Diez Barroso de Franklin 208-209 Abax, Fernando de

Haro L. • Jesús Fernández S. • Omar Fuentes E. • Bertha Figueroa P. 210 Micheas Arquitectos, Micheas Antonio

Vázquez V. 211 C Cúbica, Emilio Cabrero • Andrea Cesarman • Marco A. Coello B. 212-213 GA Grupo Arquitectura,

Daniel Álvarez F. 214-215 Arquetipo, Flavio Velázquez 218-219 MarqCó, Mariangel Álvarez • Covadonga Hernández

220-221 Terrés, Fernando Valenzuela G. • Guillermo Valenzuela G. • Javier Valenzuela G. 222-223 GLR Arquitectos,

Gilberto L. Rodríguez 224-225 Barroso Arquitectos, Ricardo Barroso 226-227 Textura®, Walter Allen 228-229

C-Chic, Olga Mussali H. • Sara Mizrahi E. 230-231 Bunker Arquitectura, Jorge Arteaga • Esteban Súarez • Sebastián

Suárez • Santiago Becerra 232-233 Abax / Patricia de Haro, Fernando de Haro L. • Jesús Fernández S. • Omar

Fuentes E. • Bertha Figueroa P. 234 JPC Arquitectos, Juan Pablo Pérez C. 235 C-Chic, Olga Mussali H. • Sara

Mizrahi E. 236-237 Extracto, Vanessa Patiño • Robert Duarte 238-239 Torbeli, Elena Talavera 240 ADI, Gina

Parlange P. 241 Abax, Fernando de Haro L. • Jesús Fernández S. • Omar Fuentes E. • Bertha Figueroa P. 242-243

Decoré Interiorismo, Maria Patricia Díaz de León 244-245 C-Chic, Olga Mussali H. • Sara Mizrahi E. 248 Agraz

Arquitectos, Ricardo Agraz O. 250-251 Arteck / Torbeli, Francisco Guzmán G. / Elena Talavera 254-255 MarqCó,

Covadonga Hernández 278-279 Terrés, Fernando Valenzela G. • Guillermo Valenzuela G. • Javier Valenzuela G.

280-281 (bottom) Abax, Fernando de Haro L. • Jesús Fernández S. • Omar Fuentes E. • Bertha Figueroa P. 286-287

CC Arquitectos, Manuel Cervantes C. • Santiago Céspedes M. 290-291 Extracto, Vanessa Patiño • Robert Duarte

292-293 Abax, Fernando de Haro L. • Jesús Fernández S. • Omar Fuentes E. • Bertha Figueroa P. 294 Garduño

Arquitectos, Juan Garduño 320-321 Grupo Diarq, Gina Diez Barroso de Franklin 322-323 Agraz Arquitectos,

Ricardo Agraz O. 326-327 Archetonic, Jacobo Micha M. 328-329 Martorell Arquitectos, Enrique Martorell

330 (top) Decoré Interiorismo, María Patricia Díaz de León (bottom) Art Arquitectos, Antonio Rueda 331 (top)

Grupo Diarq, Gina Diez Barroso de Franklin (bottom) MarqCó, Mariangel Álvarez • Covadonga Hernández

photographers
fotógrafos • photographes • fotografen

Editado en Marzo del 2010. Impreso en Tailandia.
El cuidado de edición estuvo a cargo de AM Editores S.A. de C.V.
Edited in March 2010. Printed in Thailand.
Published by AM Editores S.A. de C.V.